AF483836

God Spark

By: Caroline Vogel
Illustrated By: Rara Schlitt

Dedicated to my late grandmother
Caroline Carothers Vogel
who helped me discover the God Spark within me.

To Carrie, Marty, Bonnie, & Paige who helped me find it again.

And, Aidan, Shep, and Andy
whose God Spark I have the privilege of watching shine every day.

Author Caroline Vogel

To my grandson Mac

Illustrator Rara Schlitt

Grandma told me the **wildest** thing on Saturday!

Wild · Wild · Wild · Wild · Wild · Wild · Wild · Wild · Wild · Wild · Wild · Wild · Wild
Wild · Wild · Wild · Wild · Wild · Wild · Wild · Wild · Wild · Wild · Wild

She said that God lives *inside* me.

Love
Holy
Faith
Trinity
Harmony
Forgiveness
Story teller
Emmanuel
Shepherd
Light
Comfort
Calm
Help
Rock
ALL
Peace
Hope
Lamb
Author
Branch
Advocate
Omega
Listener
See
Lift
Guide
Refuge
Joy
Image
Counselor
Alpha
Prevail, Vision

She says there is a bright light inside me
that is a piece of God.

LIGHT

I put my hand over my belly
and my other hand over my
heart to see if I could feel
God inside me.

I waited and waited.
I wondered if maybe it might
feel like a baby **kicking** like
my little sister in
my mommy's belly.

I didn't feel anything.

That night as I laid in bed,
I looked at my night light and
thought about a bright light
being inside me.

God's light being inside
little old me.

LIGHT· LIGHT· LIGHT· LIGHT· LIGHT· LIGHT· LIGHT· LIGHT· LIGHT· LIGHT· LIGHT· LIGHT· LIGHT·

The next day I was eating dinner at Grandma's house. As Grandma and Bunny talked about grownup stuff, I sat and watched the candle light shine in the window.

And, I felt **something** in my belly.

I think I have a **flame** inside me!

Like a candle!

God's light is flickering **inside** me!

I started to wonder if people besides Grandma
could see **The Light** inside me.

As Grandma scratched my back that night, I
told her that I felt the light **inside** me.

She smiled down at me.

I could see the twinkle in her eyes. As our
eyes twinkled at each other, I thought we
might start to fly.

The next day at school I noticed the librarian
had a **pep** in her **step**. She was so excited to
share with us a new book that had arrived in
the mail.

I could see God's Spark in her eyes as she
read us the story.

27

WHOA!
LIBRARY
FUN

Mike
Tommy
Sydney
Sam
Joe
Ruth
Hazel
Art

Oh, my art teacher! How did I not see it **before?!**
God's Spark is **fireworks** in her eyes.

She gets so excited about art. It makes her
so happy to see what we make!

My teacher Mrs. Carter has the sweetest eyes.
God's Spark is like Christmas **twinkle lights**
in her eyes.

Sometimes when I get anxious, all I have to do
is look my teacher in the eye and I feel better.

Mrs Carter's Class
2ND

I noticed a girl on the playground. She seemed sad.
And, when I asked her if she was ok, she said

"I'm fine."

But, I could see God's Spark was not
very bright that day.

I didn't know what to do, so I said a quick
prayer to God.

"God, please help Sarah's spark get brighter.
I hope she feels happy soon. Amen."

I also noticed when I sat next to Andy at the lunch table, my eyes felt very **twinkly**.

Cafeteria

Bearden School Bus

When I got on the bus to go home, I noticed
the bus driver Mrs. Sharp didn't seem to have
any spark at all in her eyes.
This made me anxious.
So, I told God about it.

"God, I'm worried about Mrs. Sharp. Please
get your light going in there. *Quick!*"

Mad
Mad
Mad
Mad
Colors

I love my little brother, but sometimes
he makes me mad. Today he took my crayons
and **broke** my favorite color! I could not see
God's Spark in his eyes and I could not feel
God's light inside me.

So, I talked to God about it.

"God, I don't like feeling like this. Please help
me be able to see your *spark* in my little
brother. And, please help me feel your *light*
inside me again."

SPARK
LIGHT

Later outside I was laughing and playing with my friends. We made leaf piles and jumped in them. The more we laughed the brighter God's Spark was in all of us!

Our eyes were like fireflies in the summertime.

DANCE

The next day after school at dance class my teacher yelled at me in front of the whole class.

I felt very, very small.

I wondered if God's Spark was getting small inside me too. I didn't even know what to say to God, so I didn't tell God about it.

But, I did tell Grandma.

And, Grandma said, "Just because you feel
small doesn't mean God's Spark gets small.
And, NO ONE.
*NO ONE EVER CAN TAKE AWAY GOD'S
SPARK FROM YOU.*
Never, ever, ever."

"In fact," she said, "when you feel small you can close your eyes and imagine God's Spark inside you growing brighter and brighter. God's Spark is way brighter than anyone's words and anyone's actions."

That night as I laid in bed, I put a hand on my
belly and my other hand on my heart, and
I imagined God's Spark inside me shining as
bright as the sun on the most beautiful
beach day.

As I drifted to sleep I remembered what Grandma said,

"NO ONE EVER CAN TAKE AWAY
GOD'S SPARK FROM YOU.

Never,

ever,

ever."

The End.